IMUA
GO FORWARD

Poems of Reclamation

Puanani Burgess, Jamaica Osorio,
Kamanukea Kekoa & Noʻu Revilla

Edited by Malia Guerrero

An Imprint of Pacific University Press

Imua, Go Forward Poems of Reclamation

Published by New Ground Books, an imprint of Pacific University Press.

New Ground Books Series Editor: Dr. Kathlene Postma

Editor-in-Chief Pacific University Press: Isaac Gilman

All rights revert to the authors and artist upon publication.

Copyright © 2023 by the contributors.

Cover art by Kanani Miyamoto.

Cover and book design by Zoe Stanek.

Typography: Sanvito Pro, EB Garamond, Georgia.

Artwork featured in the book is courtesy of Kanani Miyamoto. The images are original woodcuts, linocuts, screenprints, and murals.

Printed in the United States.

ISBN 978-1-945398-13-1

For all the kids seeking themselves

DISRUPTING THE GAZE (detail)
Print installation, multiple rooms
Kanani Miyamoto

Dear Readers,

Growing up, I was never one to share the fact that I was part Hawaiian. My blonde hair, blue eyes, and fair skin also made it easy for others to assume otherwise.

Even though I danced hula for a couple of years, studied Hawaiiana throughout elementary school, and participated in summer programs centered around Hawaiian culture, I felt I wasn't allowed to embrace this part of myself. Being exposed to people who commented on my physical appearance and how I didn't fit the "image" of what a Hawaiian was supposed to look like only added to my insecurities.

By the time I graduated high school, the knowledge I once learned regarding my culture and history had vanished. My insecurity and broken connection to my Hawaiian identity had only grown stronger.

To my surprise, attending university off-island offered many opportunities for me to explore my genealogy and expand my knowledge about Hawaiian culture and history. Even though I was far from home, I had never felt more in touch with my roots.

This anthology of poems was a project that my professor proposed to me in my second year and, over the course of two years, it has come to represent my journey of reclaiming my cultural identity.

This book is by no means an end in itself. Instead, it is the beginning of a brand new journey. One in which I am able to continue learning about myself and my culture while also passing down such knowledge to future generations.

This book is for me. This book is for you.

Malia Guerrero
Editor

CONTENTS

ALOHA	13

PUANANI BURGESS — 15

'AWAPUHI	19
CHOOSING MY NAME	20
MAUNA 'ALA	21
THE MOUSE IS DREAMING	22
HE ALO A HE ALO	24
OLELO KAKOU, SISTERS (LET US SPEAK TOGETHER, SISTERS)	
E PULE KAKOU, SISTERS (LET US PRAY TOGETHER, SISTERS)	27
HAWA'I PONO 'Ī	30

JAMAICA OSORIO — 39

MAI POINA: ALOHA	42
WHEN I THINK OF EA	45
FOR NĀKO'OKO'O AND 'ULUPŌ	50
FOR MAUNA A WĀKEA	53
WE KNEW WE WERE LIBERATED WHEN WE NO LONGER FEARED FOR OUR DAUGHTERS	55
FOR MY HAUMĀNA	62
NOTES ON SURVIVING THE END OF THE WORLD, AGAIN	66

KAMANUKEA KEKOA 75
WE ARE FROM 78
H.M.S. RESOLUTION AND DISCOVERY 81
MAINLAND COLLEGE 83
LUALUALEI 85
KĪKĪWAI 88
KAIKAMAHINE 90
LOVE YOU LIKE 91

NOʻU REVILLA 97
WHEN YOU SAY "PROTESTERS" INSTEAD OF "PROTECTORS" 100
MAUNAKEA 101
THRESHOLD 103
SMOKE SCREEN 104
MEMORY AS MISSIONARY POSITION 106
INTERGENERATIONAL MEMORY 108
LESSONS IN QUARANTINE 109

ALOHA, AGAIN 118
ACKNOWLEDGEMENTS 121

ARTWORK BY KANANI MIYAMOTO 114
DISRUPTING THE GAZE 6
KA LIPO 36
MāLAMA 48

PROTECT MAUNA KEA	60
PUA	73
OJI SAN	94
CAMILLA & SERPENTS	112
SKELETON BUBBLES (detail)	116-117

ALOHA

Akahai means kindness, to be expressed with tenderness;

Lōkahi means unity, to be expressed with harmony;

'Olu'olu means agreeable, to be expressed with pleasantness;

Ha'aha'a means humility, to be expressed with modesty;

Ahonui means patience, to be expressed with perseverance.

- Pilahi Paki

The ALOHA Spirit Bill, 1986

PUANANI BURGESS

Puanani Burgess, of Native Hawaiian, Japanese, Chinese, French and German ancestry, was born in Honolulu, O'ahu in the Territory of Hawai'i in 1947. Beginning in the 1970s Aunty Pua became involved in various community struggles in Hawai'i as an advocate. She now considers herself a mediator, community developer, and facilitator of community-building and conflict transformation. Aunty Pua continues to be active in her community and beyond. She sees her work as being a cultural translator, facilitator, and transformer of conflict. She has developed transformative processes that "allow people to talk deeply to each other about things that are important to them without treating those important things as issues." She calls it "principles of building Beloved Community."

I always begin with this poem. It has done the most to teach me the difference between truth and meaning. It's funny how poets can say their own poems teach them something, but it's true.

—Puanani Burgess

'AWAPUHI

Puanani Burgess

Mama loved the scent
of wild yellow ginger,
growing thick on the slopes of Tantalus.

In its blooming season,
she would walk up that steep, curvy road
to pick two or three.

These she would weave into a brooch,
to be pinned to inside
of her blouse - hidden,
but for that warm perfume.

On the day she was buried
she wore a lei of wild yellow ginger,
freshly picked from the slopes of Tantalus,

And left for me,
in a blue shoe box,
a thousand, neatly-woven, dry,
fragrant brooches.

CHOOSING MY NAME

Puanani Burgess

When I was born my mother gave me three names:
Christabelle, Yoshie, and Puanani
Christabelle was my "English" name,
My social security card name,
My school name,
The name I gave when teachers asked me for my "real" name
A safe name

Yoshie was my home name
My everyday name,
The name that reminded my father's family
That I was Japanese, even though
My nose, hips, and feet were wide,
The name that made me acceptable to them
Who called my Hawaiian mother kuroi mame (black bean),
A saving name

Puanani is my chosen name
my piko name connecting me back to the ʻaina
And the kai and the po'e kahiko
My blessing, my burden,
My amulet, my spear

MAUNA ʻALA

Puanani Burgess

The Kaahumanu ladies, in their black lace muʻumuʻus
Wearing leis made of chicken feathers, dyed yellow,
And a boy in a blue jacket, embroidered with the words,
"HAWAIIAN INDEPENDENCE," and I are among those
who have gathered on Mauna ʻAla to mourn the passing
of Hawaiian kings and queens, princes and princesses.

We bring leis of ilima, maile, and liko lehua;
We bring prayers which all begin "O Ke Akua,"·and end in a wail;
We bring tears which we string on a long, silvery thread,
And lay these in heaps upon the concrete slabs.

        An old woman weeps as she chants:
        "Stars are buried here,
        each wrapped in a yellow wing
        of the ʻoʻo."

THE MOUSE IS DREAMING

Puanani Burgess

In a dark hole behind the washing machine
      the house-mouse is dreaming.
Whiskers, body, tail – twitching and trembling,
      paws scratching the air.
That mouse he's a dreamin
      of great chunks of cheese, and whole loaves of bread,
      of a nest made of the finest pieces of cloth and paper
          dry, warm and snug,
      of living out in the open once again, to be sun-warmed
          and star-shined,
      of walking. Of walking through the territory patrolled
          by the cats.
         of cat traps, and cat cages,
         and cats without claws and teeth;
         Of a world without cats.

And this mouse, she's a dreamin
      of acres of lo`i kalo, of nets full of `opelu,
      of rocks choked with opihi and limu,
      of forests of Koa and Iliahi and Wiliwili,
      of empty and crushing buildings which no longer

scrape the sky;
of living in the open once again, to be sun-warmed
and star-shined;
of walking. Of walking through the territory controlled
by the Cat.
of cat traps, and cat cages;
and cats without claws and teeth;
Of a world without Cats.

And the mice dream dreams
that would terrify the cat.

HE ALO A HE ALO

Puanani Burgess

He alo a he alo,
    (Face to face)

That's how you learn about what makes us weep.

He alo a he alo,
    (Face to face)

That's how you learn what makes us bleed.

He alo a he alo,
    (Face to face)

That's how you learn what makes us feel.
    what makes us work.
    what makes us sing.
    what makes us bitter.
    what makes us fight.
    what makes us laugh.
    what makes us stand against the wind
    what makes us sit in the flow of power
    what makes us, us.

Not from a distance.
Not from miles away
Not from a book
Not from an article you read
Not from the newspaper
Not from what somebody told you
Not from a "reliable source"
Not from what you think
Not from a cliff
Not from a cave
Not from your reality
Not from your darkness

But,

He alo a he alo,
      (Face to face)

Or,
else,

Pa`a kou waha.   (shut tight, your mouth)

`A`ohe o kahi nana o luna o ka pali;
iho mai a lalo nei;
`ike I ke au nui ke au iki;
he alo a he a lo.

(The top of the cliff isn't the place to look at us;
come down here and learn of the big and little current,
face to face.)

And come and help us dig, the lo`I, deep.

E ʻOLELO KAKOU, SISTERS
(LET US PRAY TOGETHER, SISTERS)

E PULE KAKOU, SISTERS
(LET US PRAY TOGETHER, SISTERS)

Puanani Burgess

Sisters and Brothers
Hear our prayer to you,

In the spirit of Aloha which our gods
bequeathed to us and
      to you,
We ask you to hear our words and
      feel our pain.

Long before your Christian forefathers
came upon our sacred ʻAina (Land),
We were three hundred thousand strong.
Strong in body, mind and spirit.
Our gods, our ways, our ʻaina, our sea and sky
provided and nourished us.

But your forefathers came to our shores
they brought with them the Cross and

the Flag, and
Disease, and
Alcohol, and
Despair, and
Greed, and
Shame for what we were - "lowly heathens"
(I think they said).

They offered, no, demanded,
that we accept the Cross and the Flag
    (these Siamese twins of Power)
And said, "Here. With these you will prosper."

We tried to put into their hands, our symbols:
    The Kalo, (taro) from whose body we take sacred nourishment.
    The 'aina, from whose body we take sacred nourishment.
    The Wai and the Kai, (the inland and sea Water) from
whose body we take sacred nourishment

But they scorned our symbols, They scorned us.
They said, "Here. With these, you will prosper."

But look at us now, Sisters.
    We are the poorest.
    We live in cars, tents, on benches and sidewalks.
    We occupy more jail cells, more hospital beds, more morgue
        slabs and coffins
Than any other race in Hawaii.
Our children are labelled "DISADVANTAGED" and can't read
                                      can't write
                                      can't get a job
                                      can't get an education.

We are beggars in our own homeland.

But no more.
As we lay down the Cross,
As we lay down the Flag,
We search and have found those symbols which spring from this place
                                                             this time
                                                             this People.

In our hands we offer you
        a scoop of earth, the ʻAina
        a scoop of water from the land and the sea, Life
        a rainbow, Hope
        and Aloha, Love.

But let us be clear.
Whether you accept our symbols
        or not,
We will continue to speak the truth of our history
                the truth of our pain
                the truth of our oppression
                the truth of our colonization.
And through this truth we will be free.

This is our prayer to you, sisters.
Listen to it with your soul, sisters.

                Amene.

HAWAI'I PONO 'Ī

Puanani Burgess

On Friday, August 7, 1987
Forty-three kanakas from Wai`anae,
In a deluxe, super-duper, air-conditioned, tinted-glass
        tourist-kind bus,
Headed to Honolulu on an excursion to the Palace,
        `Iolani Palace.

Racing through Wai`anae, Ma`ili, Nānākuli—
Past Kahe Point, past the `Ewa Plain—
In the back of the bus, the teenagers – 35 of them
Rappin', and snappin', and shouting to friends and strangers
        Alike: Eh, howzit, check it out, goin' to town...

(Along the way, people stop and stare, wondering,
        What are those blahs and titas doing in that bus?)

Cousin Bozo, our driver, (yes, that's his real name)
Spins the steering wheel, turning the hulk-of-a-bus,
Squeezing and angling it through the gates made just
Wide enough for horses and carriages and buggies.

Docent Doris greets us:
"Aloha mai. Aloha mai. Aloha mai.

"Only twenty per group, please.
'Young people, please, deposit your gum and candy in the trash.
"No radios. No cameras.
"Quiet. Please."

"Now, will you all follow me up these steps.
"Hele mai `oukou e `āwīwī."

Like a pile of fish, we rushed after her.

At the top of the steps,
We put on soft, mauve colored cloth coverings over our
      shoes and slippers,
         to protect the precious hard wood floors
         from the imprint of our modern step.

Through the polished koa wood doors, with elegantly etched
      glass windows,
Docent Doris ushers us into another Time.
Over the carefully polished floors we glide, through the
      darkened hallways: spinning, sniffing, turning,
         fingers reaching to touch something sacred, something forbidden
      – quickly.

Then into the formal dining room, silent now.
Table set: the finest French crystal gleaming; spoons,
      knives, forks, laid with precision next to gold-rimmed
      plates with the emblem of the King.
Silent now.

La`amea `Ū.

Portraits of friends of Hawa`i line the dining room walls:
> a Napoleon, a British Admiral ... But no portrait of
> any American President. (Did you know that?)

Then, into the ballroom,
Where the King, Kalākaua, and his Queen, Kapi`olani, and their
> guests
> waltzed, sang and laughed and yawned into the dawn.
> (No one daring to leave before His Majesty)

The Royal Hawaiian Band plays
> the Hawaiian National Anthem and all chattering
> and negotiating stops. As the King and his shy Queen
> descend the center stairway.

And up that same stairway, we ascend – the twenty of us.
Encouraged, at last, to touch ...
> Running our hands over the koa railing,
> ... we embrace our history.

To the right is the Queen's sunny room ... a faint
> rustle of petticoats.

To the left, we enter the King's study:

> Books everywhere. Photographs everywhere.
> The smell of leather, and tobacco, ink and parchment –
> The smell of a man at work.

> Electric light bulbs (in the Palace of a savage,
> can you imagine?)
> Docent Doris tells us to be proud, that electricity lit
> the Palace before the White House.

>   There, a telephone on the wall.

>   Iwalani longs to open those books on his desk,
>   Tony tries to read and translate the documents,
>   written in Hawaiian, just lying on his desk.

La`amea `Ū.

Slowly, we leave the King.
And walk into the final room to be viewed on the
        second floor.
The room is almost empty; the room is almost dark.
It is a small room. It is a confining room.
            It is the prison room of Queen Lili`uokalani.

Docent Doris tells us:

"This is the room Queen Lili`uokalani was imprisoned in
for eight months, after she was convicted of treason.
She had only one haole lady-in-waiting.
She was not allowed to leave this room during that
time;
She was not allowed to have any visitors or
communications with anyone else;
She was not allowed to have any knowledge of what was
happening to her Hawai`i or to her people."

Lili`uokalani `Ū.

I move away from the group.
First, I walk to one dark corner, then another,
    then another. Pacing. Pacing, Searching.

        Trying to find a point of reference, an anchor,
        a hole, a door, a hand, a window, my breath ...
I was in that room. Her room. In which she lived and
        died and composed songs for her people. It was
        the room in which she composed prayers to a
        deaf people:

        "Oh honest Americans, hear me for my downtrodden
        people ..."

She stood with me at her window;
Looking out on the world, that she would never rule again;
Looking out on the world that she would only remember
        in the scent of flowers;
Looking out on a world that once despised her,

And in my left ear, she whispered:
E, Pua. Remember:

This is not America.
And we are not Americans.

Hawa`I Pono`Ī.

Amene.

KA LIPO
Print Installation
Kanani Miyamoto
Photo by Mel Carter

The Kumulipo, a Hawaiian creation story, has been a great influence on my work. The ideas and thoughts that come from this Hawaiian creation chat are numerous. I'm inspired by the scientific logic and documentation, the poetics and metaphors, and the ideas of connectivity and interdependence embedded in the oli.

I've done work thinking about the how our ancestors viewed the darkness that everything was created from. A deep dark blue blackness. They describe this blackness with respect and reverence and explain that the darkness from the deepest parts of the ocean is where life first emerges. Contrary to western beliefs where darkness is viewed as negative, Kānaka Maoli recognized the beauty in the dark unknown.

—Kanani Miyamoto

JAMAICA OSORIO

Dr. Jamaica Heolimeleikalani Osorio is a Kanaka Maoli wahine artist / activist / scholar / storyteller born and raised in Pālolo Valley to parents Jonathan and Mary Osorio. Jamaica earned her Ph.D. in English (Hawaiian literature) from the University of Hawai'i at Mānoa. Currently, Jamaica is an Assistant Professor of Indigenous and Native Hawaiian Politics at the University of Hawai'i at Mānoa. Jamaica is a three-time national poetry champion, poetry mentor, and published author. Her poetry and activism are the subjects of an award-winning film, *This is the Way we Rise*. She was a lead artist and co-writer of the revolutionary VR Documentary, *On the Morning You Wake (To the end of the world)*. A proud past Kaiāpuni student, Jamaica is a graduate of Kamehameha, Stanford University (BA), and New York University (MA). Her book *Remembering our Intimacies: Mo'olelo, Aloha 'Āina, and Ea* was published by The University of Minnesota Press.

MAI POINA: ALOHA

Jamaica Osorio

The haole say:
Aloha means goodbye,
But you and I know better
Instead,
Aloha is the way i say:
i am always with you, even when you choose to leave
Aloha is the way i say:
you used to live outside of me
And now, i feel you etched into my every breath
Aloha is the way i say:
I've pulled mountains out of the sea to bring forth the world you deserve
Because Aloha is the spell i whisper into ever gourd i can find,
Hoping it calls the right wind to bring you back to me
Aloha is what brings you back to me

Aloha is what i say,
because it is the only word audacious enough to try to hold you
And aloha reminds me
Thats there is no word for goodbye in our language
Our kupuna have no map for me to understand
this kind of departure

So instead I say
I love you
Even when you are walking away
I say,
I am waiting for the day we are we again
I say
There is a dance between wahine like me and you
Its as natural as the tide's insistence to rise

Aloha reminds me:
I want to speak to you the way our kupuna would
With language pulled out of this dirt, fished from our sea
I want you to know
What i mean
When i say:
We are a mo'olelo i heard long ago but never had the courage to believe
& today aloha is choosing bravery for me

E ku'u wahine aloha.
Eia au e kū nei me ke aloha pau 'ole
Me he 'a'ali'i kū makani mai la
'a'ohe mea nāna e kūla'i
E ho'i mai, a mo'olelo nō kāua
I mea e kono i ka 'oia'i'o mai kēia pō mai
Mai poina
'o 'oe no ka'u i upu ai
Mai poina
'o 'oe nō, he lei mau no ku'u kino
Mai poina

A hui pū hou nō kāua
Mai poina

Aloha.

WHEN I THINK OF EA

Jamaica Osorio

One.

When I think of ea
I think of music
The breath breaking off the roof of my fathers mouth
How its the softest broken i known
I think of the makani
The way it must carry its own memory
I think of the way both
My father
The wind of his voice
How my first practice in visioning came through singing
In the malu of my father's mountain range shoulders
Under the breath of his wai'ōma'o winds
How I would do anything to protect him

Two.
When I think of sacrifice
I think about led cut against its will
I think of the bodies, something like a pōhaku
Forced into small shapes to paint death on my 'āina
On my people
I think of the way Pōhakuloa sings her own song

In the dead of night
Shakes us awake in her trembling

Three.
When I think of ʻeha
I see his face again
In his dark blues
I think of the ocena that must still connect us
But there are too many weapons between us to recognize our pilina
When i think of ʻeha
I think of
Clenched jaws and tears streaming like rivers
Across skin the same tint as my own
I think of my voice
Reaching out to him
"Brother, stand with us"
I think,
In another time
We stood on the same side
I think,
Mauna a Wākea also casts her malu of protection on him
I think,
That makes us family
I believe,
next time we will be facing the same direction

Four.
When I think of trust
I remember my mothers fingertips
Dancing across my back

The way the shore break dances upon the sand
I think of all the ways
Love is a verb, a choice, a memory we hold on to

When I think of trust
I think of my fists
And everything i've lost to them
All the sand, salt and promises that crept out from between long fingertips
How I am not so much like my mother
The grace of her open hands
That can hold so much without suffocating
All the breath around her
How she never fails to make the wind dance

Five.
When I think of ea
I wonder
What will I offer back to my lāhui
With fists full of rocks
All their breath, all squeezed out
With name im still learning to recall

MāLAMA
Wood block print
Kanani Miyamoto

Hula and mele are integral to Hawaiian culture. Hula is a sacred practice a powerful space and time continum. Connecting the dancer to the ancestors who sang and danced the same songs. Connecting the dancer to the place of origin dancing with strong bear feet. Transporting the witnesses of the hula with them while they dance. The hula dancer spends countless hours learning songs lyrics and meaning. The dancer spends countless hours practicing getting every movement just right. The dancers adorn themselves with kupe'e; lei for the head, hands, feet. These adornments are picked from the forests or sea, but not without permission and an offering of an oli. Hula and mele connects us to our ancestors, hula and mele connect us to the place of our origin.

—Kanani Miyamoto

FOR NĀKO'OKO'O AND 'ULUPŌ

Jamaica Osorio

In an empty church house
We remembered
Together
All the abundance that never forgot us
We sat as the night grew deeper around us
Until we could feel creation again

And when the morning arrived
With her heat
We gathered:
      Our courage
      Our kupuna,
      Our hopes,
      and inspirations
We honored these moments by singing
Mele into an 'Āina that never forgot our ea

And with our lima turned down
And our mo'olelo churning between us
We grew:

      Lo'i
      'ike,
      kaiāulu,
      AND each other
Until we overflowed
Mud between our toes and
Laughter spilling over our lips

And when we were weak,
unsure of our words and footing
We leaned into the unknown and each other
Found aloha in the sturdy offering of a hand, a shoulder,
a quiet, but reassuring sigh

We brought the 'ulukoa back to the kai at oneawa
Storming our bodies across kailua beach
Our brown skins shimmering in the shore break
The sky opened itself above us
Nodding in her approval
Welcoming us back home

So when Malia asked us to
Share a time we fell deeper in love with our lāhui
Each and everyone of us had too many examples that come to mind
We scrubbed words on a whiteboard that taunted us in christian scripture

And so today as we we remove our trace
from the hale that held us
We carefully wash every corner clean

leaving only the verses of our aloha, inscribed
Color expo ink carving our memory into another white background
Another kailua, waikīkī, University of Hawai'i,
Another place that been transformed to insist we do not belong
That tells us that we are too brash,
our 'ike too native,
our grief to deep,
our joy too loud...
        too strong, too kanaka to be right

But today we practice the ancient resistance of staying
We leave our Mo'olelo
A simple and insistent reminder
that no one can ignore

FOR MAUNA A WĀKEA

Jamaica Osorio

Its been 300 days since I first laid in your arms
First felt the chill of your kiss on my skin
You brought me to the thin line between life and death
Between frostbite and heat exhaustion
You taught me balance
Patience
Compassion

And when you stretched your arms around us
You taught us safety
What it meant to create securities from our own bodies
Voices
So for you
I am every child who imagined someday you'd be free
I am every prayer laid at your feet

These days
I am hundreds of miles away
But you still visit me in my dreams
We share ceremony with Niolopua

And in that realm
You keep all my secrets
All my fears
All I am too afraid or ashamed to say out loud

For my fellow kia'i
Its been 300 days since we marked the boundaries
Lined our jurisdictions with the trembling tenor of our collective voice
Since we began to feed each other
In food
In spirit
In care

For you
I am everything that cannot be broken
I am your first pinky promise
I am the incoming swell
I am every bit of love you taught me to lay at her feet
I am songs between stories, between tears
I am the water we fought to protect
That we shared
Together
In the bitter cold of night
When we worried
No one else was coming

WE KNEW WE WERE LIBERATED WHEN WE NO LONGER FEARED FOR OUR DAUGHTERS

Jamaica Osorio

Its been raining for days
the kind where the sky turns grey
and you wonder if it'll ever turn back
its 53 degrees in Hawai'i (which is really fucking cold, btw)
and my 6-week-old daughter is sneezing more than usual
My partner looked it up
Some babies sneeze when they are cold
so i am holding them both a little closer than normal
which is pretty damn close

at night
i close the windows
I warp her in a lei of blankets
i say her name
out loud
remind her that she is loved

safe

o wau no kou kia'i

I am your protector

i say

over and over until she will be ready to say it back

and her mother and i wait to hear her fall asleep

and then we settle into each-other

this is the future we dreamed of, together

from the frontlines of a movement protecting our mountain, our water, each other

and it is full of everything sweet, and beautiful, and tender

but we are no longer in a pu'uhonua

so it is also overflowing with everything i fear

The US navy is poisoning the water in Hawai'i

tens of thousands of gallons of diesel fuel have already spilled into our aquifer

250 million gallons remain in these WWII single wall degrading tanks

and the Navy is refusing to drain and decommission them

even after admitting to the contamination

on twitter and Instagram I see photo ops with "the best" of congressional leaders handing out

bottled water and hotel vouchers to military service families

like band aids on a bullet wound

and for the first time in my life

I feel completely helpless

There is an invisible plume of poison working its way through our underground water systems

And the only people who know the exact extent of it

Don't give a fuck about us
Our 'āina and wai, and certainly think nothing of our children
In fact, while preparing a suit against our state for demanding they drain the tanks the US NAVY
insists: "It is not the fuel in the tanks, but the fuel in the water that's making us sick"
Let me say that again
The US navy says: "its not the fuel in their tanks, but the fuel in OUR water that is making us
sick"
And I give no fucks about their lyrical gymnastics
There is no rewriting themselves out of fault

I want to ask them
how will i feed my daughter if all we have is jet fuel falling from the faucet
instead I start googling DYI home rain catchments
while I spin into a tornado of my own fear
I can only think about the decades our people have been calling to demilitarize our island and
ocean
and how no one beyond our lāhui cared to listen

and now it's the TV and twitter and Instagram all popping off
and the water is rising
and the Covid variants are multiplying
and there are guns and cops and cages everywhere
and my checking account is hemorrhaging money
and my daughter is crying
and it hasn't stopped raining
its been days

and it's true, i used to long for these moments
a quality storm to quiet my house and mind
me in a corner with a pen and pad of paper
but today
i have a sneezing daughter in my arms
and i know that means she is cold
so i am holding her a little closer than normal
which is pretty damn close
and i cant stop thinking about how little I can protect her
and now I know I am really a mother of a daughter
because i am made only of worry

and i am thinking about water
the wai that is now fuel
and the kai that is still rising
all around us
and the mud that is creeping closer and closer to my doorway
with each day that the deluge continues

and i am waiting for someone to come and hold me
to tell me i am loved
to say that at least for today the water is safe
I am waiting for someone to remind me that we too are worth protecting
like a mauna, like an island, like our ocean, expanding

i look into my daughter's eyes again
o wau no kou kia'i
I am your protector
she says

first to the ʻāina, then to the wai, and finally to me
and for a moment
I can breathe again
Because at the very least
Malia and I did one thing right

We prepared one more wahine koa to take into battle
But I cannot help but think
is this really as far as we can dream?

PROTECT MAUNA KEA
Screen Print
Kanani Miyamoto

This poster was made at the start of the Mauna Kea movement. While living in Portland, OR I felt it may kuelana to make and distribute these posters to bring awareness of Native Hawaiian issues back home.

—Kanani Miyamoto

FOR MY HAUMĀNA

Jamaica Osorio

Remember the year we spent in pō?
How all the things we thought we learned came back up
Again
And again
And again
As if there was something we missed?
But couldn't quite catch
We spent days holding our breath turning our heads in circles until our faces were blue

Remember those months we spent grieving
Sitting in our darkness
Forgetting the light
Mourning a life
That seemed so far away
We questioned if it even happened?

Remember how we (d)evolved
How we became a string of ones and zeros
Represented in high definition
But still
Carved out to fit in binary

In someone else's algorithm
Living our lives in 75 minute increments

Remember all the mele we lost
How we forgot how to sing in harmony
or at least in unison
How we sat there in our own void
Silent
Constantly facing our disconnection
When you reached out for pilina
Do Remember the thumbnails that starred back at you?
How you wondered if you would ever know the tenor of their sighs

Or the emails
Remember the endless strings of emails
One after the other
Each a reminder that
No one seems to have escaped this heaviness
This flood
This deluge
How your haumāna
Endured challenges you cannot even imagine
Losses you dont know how to hold or comfort
All from behind the lonely blue glow of a computer monitor
Hearts trembling
Hands hovering over the unmute button
Stuck
Remember how your employer did give a fuck
And insisted you evaluate them with a letter grade anyway
How the failures of "leadership" soon began to not surprise

As the body count continued to rise

Remember How so many times you wished
You could reach out to them
Your students
With more than an arm of an email thread
With more than
Ke aloha nō
How many times you wondered if they felt your sincerity
Or if it had been distorted through the microphone
Caught and lost somewhere in the endless ether lodged between you

I dont think I will ever forget
The way this silence broke us like a flood summer rain
Like a storm shaking us from the summit
Just like we wont forget how we survived still
Beside each other
Even Thousands of miles away
The lines of mana wahine we endured to create
Armed held out taut across the oceans and continents
Made something old
Almost familiar
Out of something so strange, distant
And inhumane

Most of all I wonder what will remain
Will they know
My haumāna
How I wished so much more for us
For them, for sure

How most nights I stayed awake paralyzed by our collective anxiety
How I wanted to show them this ʻāina that has loved and made me
How I wanted to turn our hands together, down to her
So they might have the chance to be loved
And made again too

But instead
What we have together is this pō
This dark and churning heat
Still expanding, growing around us
Into something I dont know how to hold
All we have is this quiet between us
And the knowing that something better
or simply something else is soon coming

NOTES ON SURVIVING THE END OF THE WORLD, AGAIN

Jamaica Osorio

On the morning you wake to the end of the world

take your body back to the kai
to the place our kūpuna taught us life began
first pō, then coral, then slime
then a whole universe fitting into a space smaller than a grain of sand
then Ea rising through the ocean
pulling the tides that make mountains
valleys, and the rivers that cut through them
Remember our ʻāina
for all the ways that she has fed us
in the quiet darkness
before the blast
dive yourself back into the depth of creation
recalling all the times your world has ended before:

Call out the names of all the violence that has come

While calling itself protection
All the ways we have been left
To gather the shattered pieces
Two island cities in the corner of the pacific
Flattened to caricature
Names rendered meaningless,
Carved over and over again into the binding of our textbooks
Just enough of their shape remains to call foul at our hubris
But does nothing to slow the arrogant push of "progress"
In their toxic wake
Came our "Imperial Lake"
Our grand Moana Nui Cut wide open

So on the morning you wake to the end of the world,
Chant all of the names of our dead and dying
Refuse to forget:
        Kahoʻolawe, Mākua, Pōhakuloa, Mokoliʻi

And then look to the horizon
Call upon the memory of hundreds tests
Carried across our oceanic backs

Bikini and Ānewetak,
Kiritimati and Kalama,
Meralinga and Emu,
Moruroa and Fang ata ufa
And all the unnamed caught choking downwind
Epili Hauʻofa's beautiful Sea of Islands vison perverted into a sea of toxic waste
The enduring gift from our American, British and French "protectorates"

So on the morning you wake to the end of the world
Remember,
we have lived this ending before
Each bomb of history its own strike
The coming of ships
The spreading of death
The taming of industry
The carving of land, crosses, and cultures
Until all that was left
Is what could be packaged and sold back at a premium

All because the men with the plans called power
Promised us "security" behind the barrel of a gun
Cut a fortress out of a breadbasket and called it "productive"
Warships, cannons, and Gatling guns pointed at the palace
Then fixed into the 'iwi of our mountains
For "protection"
None of it
Will save us the violence that will continue to come
Bullets only beget more bullets
Bombs only beget bigger bombs
And in the end, all we are left with is this waste,
Waiting.

And still all this death
Is not enough to force our forgetting
Our water, our moana, has a memory
And we are made in her image
Together

Meaning
we are
intimately connected
and infinitely powerful
so who but ourselves can hold us accountable?
When none of what has been built will save us
From what cannot be called back

Remember
This mo'olelo:
The ea of change is heat
The ea of life only rises from ʻāina and kai
There is no part of you that is meant to survive
When the cost is this place
Perched up as collateral damage
America's shining shield sitting in the heart of the pacific
A warning blast calling for what's next

Know this:
On the morning you wake to the end of the world
your vision will be 20-20
so use it
as the men with the "plans" called power call out from behind their
screens to tell you to take cover
see beyond the violence of their contradiction
the enduring waste of their direction
call upon your own mana to make a change

Choose to remember
Our ʻāina, this kai, these kuahiwi

And all they have witnessed
Even more they have endured
And still stand to protect us,
Follow their wisdom
Come Armageddon or high water
hold them close
Pull a pule from our na'au
Call out to your akua by name
And commit to live your life in their image
Not matter what the consequence
And maybe
Just maybe
The world may not have to end again
Tomorrow

These prints were inspired by the spiritual practice of hula and Hawaiians' deep connection to land.

—Kanani Miyamoto

PUA
Wood block print
Kanani Miyamoto

KAMANUKEA KEKOA

Kamanukea Kekoa is a music and Hawaiian history teacher at Waolani Judd Nazarene School on Oʻahu, Hawaiʻi. Her hopes for this anthology is to encourage and inspire readers, especially her students, to find their voice and raise it for what they believe in.

She writes: "Born in the arms of the Koʻolau, Kapālama sheltered me for most of my life. When I was allowed to choose my own path, Kaʻala led me home and Lualualei embraces me each morning. Melodies were my first language, and poetry flowed as a result. There is much I don't know, and much to learn, and while I never intended anyone to see these, I offer my love for Hawaiʻi on these pages. He kanaka ʻoiwi au, he pulapula i ka malu o Ka Haku au, he lālā a Lanakila au, he pua onaona o Leinaʻala au, nāu nō me ke aloha."

WE ARE FROM

Kamanukea Kekoa

i am from rocks
that which holds my culture
because it is, i am
the small pebbles on a kōnane board
the foundation of the kuapā
the sibling boulders resting in Hāʻena
the koʻa that forms all life
ua lawa mākou i ka pōhaku, i ka ʻai kamahaʻo o ka ʻāina
I come from strength, from solidity
from Consciousness, Awareness is born
e ola nā pōkahu no laila e ola mau

i am from trees
that which holds my culture
because it is, i am
the ʻulu of Kū that ended famine
the trunk carved into kiʻi and waʻa
the fish charming branch Mākālei
the ever deepening roots clinging to soil
i ulu no ka lālā i ke kumu
i come from growth, from resiliency
from Consciousness, Awareness is born

e ola nā kumulāʻau no laila e ola mau
i am from flowers
that which holds my culture
because it is, i am
the messages carried by the blooms of Paoakalani
the separated naupaka lovers
the lehua blossoms strung in a lei poʻo
the koʻoloaula tucked behind my ear
mohala i ka wai ka maka o ka pua
i come from beauty, from virility
from Consciousness, Awareness is born
e ola nā pua no laila e ola mau

i am from fresh water
that which holds my culture
because it is, i am
the droplet held in the piko of a kalo leaf
the spring thrusted from the earth by Kāne's staff
the re-diverted streams of Maui that flow freely
the shrouding mists embracing lovers in Waimea
aia i laila ka wai a Kāne, he wai e mana
i come from wealth, from fluidity
from Consciousness, Awareness is born
e ola nā wai no laila e ola mau

we are from Hawai'i
the stars our maps
the birds our songs
the winds and rains our books
because it is, we are

connected by ʻāina
cemented by aloha
sustained by pono
we are Hawaiʻi
ke hoʻohiki nei au i koʻu kupaʻa ma hope o koʻu lahui
na kanaka maoli o keia aina nei
e hoʻomanaʻo mau ana au no na kau a kau
i recognize myself in the water
i give myself in the flowers
i see myself in the trees
i find myself in the rocks

H.M.S. RESOLUTION AND DISCOVERY

Kamanukea Kekoa

There is a young woman wearing a dress looking at me from the other side of this ship. Her eyes crinkle in confusion, as do mine. I did not see her arrive, nor hear her. She vaguely reminds me of a watery someone. The sun plays tricks on me when i see my grandmothers eyes.

I sit up straighter to get a better look and she moves at the same moment. Our faces twist in surprise. She is not from this ʻāina because I do not think that I know her.

We smile at each other and her brown eyes fill with the same aloha i feel brimming in my heart for her. What was she doing here too? She should not be here too.

The white skinned sailor barks what feels like a command and I break my gaze as I so graciously receive a handful of hard edged metal stones.

I settle back to stare out at the ocean, my familiar blue,
comparing the gentle sea spray to roiling shore breaks.
My mouth waters in yearning for the sweet juice of a tender niu,
quenching parched throats from swallowing sand and coral shards.

This strange boats' boards creeks and sails clanks.
A canoe ride is much smoother.

Koaʻe cries ahead and the woman and I turned our heads up. Is it time
to go back now? We rise at the same time, longing rises up in me to hold
that young woman, convince her why she should never come back to this
place. I will remind her of fragrant kapa, dew laden palaʻā, tree trunk ʻūhā
and twisted maile, shady afternoons and moonlit mornings.

In two strides we are face to face. I know this woman.
I've seen that ʻehu hair splayed down shoulders and stubby fingers
wrapped around pohaku kuʻi ʻai. I've seen those silt colored shins and
that sun shaped scar on her sternum. We reach out and our veins match,
identical wrinkles mark a pathway home.
Recognition flows from her cool palm, my cool palm.
I pull my hand away as I try to make sense of this solid pool,
of how I can stand here yet she stands there
I stand here and she stands there we stand here.
Tears spring to my eyes as I exhale a sigh of relief.
She was ok, she was fine.
She could go back to bare feet running and ʻiʻiwi feathers and
forget about slippery puhi and salty stinging eyes and
embrace ʻoʻopu suckers and honu nests.
It was just me.

MAINLAND COLLEGE

Kamanukea Kekoa

Slow morning starting
Airplane rising
New beginnings
Rays streaming through misty clouds
Tears streaming down brown cheeks
Your face is turned towards the sun

This flying island is much more metal than ours
The bitterness of P.o.G. seeps in the spaces of my gums
I don't understand why you're doing this
This is my chance for a better life
Life is better here at home
Home is too damn small
Youre too damn small

You are a kahuli
Wrapped up in your own arms
Peering out from your shell
Looking for the
Next leaf
To take you to your
Next step
My how many steps youve taken

How far you've come
Come from my memory

Turbulence jolts my attention away from my memory
You are still looking out the window
The wing of the airplane an extension of your own.
I'm sorry, I'm just going to miss you
You'll be ok
Ok isn't good enough
I'm coming back soon
Soon is so far away
You know i'll miss you too. I promise

You are a koholā
gliding north
fins stretched wide riding the current
Looking for the
Next island
To take you to your
Next step
When seasons change and you fly south
Again

Quick evening finishing
Our plane descending
Old endings
Rays setting behind the Koʻolau thousands of miles away
Tears streaming down brown cheeks
Your back is turned from the sea
Eia Hawaiʻi…E hoʻi mai…
Home is waiting

LUALUALEI

Kamanukea Kekoa

E Lualualei, Eō mai, E hō mai
My hands curl deep into you
Trying to give you life
While in fact it is you who
Sustains me
Breathes me
Keeps me

How could anyone understand what you mean to me
What you give me
How you make me live
How I yearn for you to live
Again

E Lualualei, you have been my constant morning
Promises born of the pregnant darkness come to life
as i witness your sky change
the black behind my eyes opening ka lā o ka lā
Sunlight paints ʻāina, traced on the whorls of my naʻau
When Kānehoalani rises and rays rest on your shoulders,
peace inundates dry bones.
When Hinahānaiakamalama sets behind Paheʻeheʻe,

warmth courses through chilled veins.
When i touch your soil for the first time,
passion permeates my ribs
And only when all is pono do my wings unsheath themselves from my back as I stretch, release, break free. You call. I am awake.

E Lualualei, you have been my unwavering teacher
You taught me to look for myself in the soil stained creases of my hands
My feet learned your name as you whispered, begging me to hear you
"Help me help you. I have so much to give. Let me feed you."
So i've become a Farmer
He mahi'ai au
Pono nō au e mahi
I cant feel you at my desk
I cant hear you on the bus
I cant see you under concrete
Lualualei, I cant touch you if I dont try
So I mahi because I must
You taught. I am listening.

E Lualualei, you have been my pathway home
Your vast valleys encircled me
as I watched the clouds make shapes on your back
like arms holding me, protecting me
Pūhāwai bursting with proof that our ancestors chose you wisely
Ka'ala in the distance sending 'iwa when ive lost my way,
when I forgot how to use my wings
The current at Ma'ili a refreshing reminder that
home is where youve chosen to plant your roots
And i am clinging to your virile lepo

Reaching further down to the blueprints of your existence
Before the development, Beyond their disregard, Beneath destruction
You are there.
Restoration creation reparation
Waiting to welcome me home.
You embrace. I am ready

One day I will see my son trimming the branches of his aunty's koa tree
One day I will help my daughter braid the kupukupu into a lei
One day I will save you from the selfish monsters
who leave hundreds of your acres barren
One day I will lay my iwi to rest beneath your starry gaze
One day starts today. You give. I am full.

E Lualualei, you are not static, you are continuous.
You were here before me and you will remain long after.
With the legacy i have been entrusted, i will be a constant morning.
I will be an unwavering teacher. I will show them the pathway home.
Mahalo. Mahalo. Mahalo.

Keep me
breathe into me
sustain me
it is you
give me life
curl around my hands
e hō mai, eo mai, E Lualualei

KĪKĪWAI

Kamanukea Kekoa

aloha e kuu kamaaina
child of the land
the accustomed is by you
food belonging to the child
to pry against what is stuck
familiar, native born
welcome home
i have been waiting for you
waiting to lick at the hairs of your arm
for my coldness to creep against your clavicle
to hold your head in my waves
i have been waiting for you
thousands of foreign toes try to jam themselves
into the grooves and arches your feet have shaped
i languish in the gentle steps, prints that know where they are going each
stride carefully taken and i place each mossy rock to lead you
i have missed your awareness, thoughtfulness,
understanding about my fragile state
yearning for the love you leave in each droplet
the first full submersion brings you to me
i dance through the strands, nourish them back to life
i race across your skin, aching to cover ever inch, claim you as mine.
Wrinkle your fingers to grasp my currents.

i kiss your eye lashes, your fingernails, your lower back
dive deeper, deep, the deep breathes, breath is deep
welcome home

KAIKAMAHINE

Kamanukea Kekoa

4 little brown girls playing on the street
filipino man zooms over ones feet
Aunty said that uncle said we no can eat
3 little brown girls playing on the street

3 little brown girls jumping in the street
haole teacher kicks one out, "she cheats"
Aunty said that uncle said we no can eat
2 little brown girls jumping in the street

2 little brown girls hiding in the street
kepani uncle purrs to clutch ones pleats
Aunty said that uncle said we no can eat
1 little brown girl hiding in the street

1 little brown girl sleeping in the street
Kanaka officer scoops her in the backseat
He slides a snickers through the grate
How long she never eat
  10 more brown girls sleeping in the street

LOVE YOU LIKE

Kamanukea Kekoa

Aloha nō ia ʻāina a ke onaona i noho ai
He hone mai hoʻi kau a koe
He ʻiʻini kau nō ka manaʻo

i had never noticed the ocean in her eyes before
koholā diving out of sight,
and like an ʻupena upon my face
her eyelashes catch my breath and i can't look away.

i had never noticed the earth in her eyes before
ʻaʻaliʻi capsules fallen on soil,
and like an ʻōʻō to the chest
the layers of desire break apart and the roots are laid.

had never noticed the fire in her eyes before
Kukui oil dripping down my fingers,
and like fire brands whipped across the sky
Let the world know you are mine and I am yours.

i had never noticed the clouds in her eyes before
pigs and dogs shifting back and forth,

and like the underbelly of a lono billow
catalytic winds carried you away.

I had never noticed the river in her eyes before
'opae darting between smooth pohaku
and like an o'opu returning upstream
she's gone before i realize my heart went with her.

He ali'i ka 'āina
He kauā ke kanaka

OJI SAN
Print installation
Kanani Miyamoto

This work was a personal reflection and a reconnection to my Japanese heritage. It was at this time I really started to embrace and appreciate what intersectionality is and means.
—Kanani Miyamoto

NOʻU REVILLA

Noʻu Revilla (she/her) is an ʻŌiwi poet, performer, and educator. Born and raised with the Līlīlehua rain of Wai'ehu on the island of Maui, she currently lives and loves with the Līlīlehua rain of Pālolo valley on O'ahu. Her debut book of poetry *Ask the Brindled* was selected by Rick Barot as a winner of the 2021 National Poetry Series. She has performed and facilitated workshops throughout Hawai'i and abroad. She is an assistant professor of creative writing at the University of Hawai'i-Mānoa and a lifetime "slyly / reproductive" student of Haunani-Kay Trask.

WHEN YOU SAY "PROTESTERS" INSTEAD OF "PROTECTORS"

Noʻu Revilla

I would call it a trick, if it wasn't so terrifying, the way your mouth doesn't move when you speak. Your smile, shiny as a church, but what kind of prayer could ever be trusted without evidence of a free tongue? On the rare occasion sound shakes loose, words, no matter how unmuzzled, words still go to die. In your mouth, even womb is wound. Sometimes I dream of tearing your throat wide open and finding there, where stories should be born, only bleeding bleedingbleeding. The wish to desecrate. We are, yet again, portrayed by you, ~~the girl~~ ~~the Native~~ ~~the water~~ the mountain who was "asking for it." Your lips so Sunday still. Sometimes I almost believe you. So it's best I keep hiding knives in my hair, the way my grandmother – not god – the way my grandmother intended.

MAUNAKEA

No'u Revilla

Inside me: two seeds.
One planted in my throat,

a dark highway fingered
by akua moonlight.

The other seed raised
in a fist of bright veins.

Who will taste without swallowing
my grove of lehua?

In a world terrified of rain,
who will kiss my resilient

red mouth? 'O wai kou kupunahine?
I carry these seeds like a child

carries her grandmother's blood.
'O ka 'āina nō. 'O ka 'āina nō.

Trucks are still carrying medicine
folding tables & hot food,

water   water
water   water

and the faithful still drive the dark
highway to ke ala hulu kupuna,

where the sky is so thin,
thinnest of all skins come to stitch

a new story, so thin I can see bone.
from seed to summit, our bones matter.

'O wai kou kupunahine?
'O ka 'āina nō. 'O ka 'āina no.

THRESHOLD

Noʻu Revilla

a mass stranding   *I could not deliver the poem*   the Navy determined that vessels involved in training&testing might strike&kill endangered blue whales   *I could never find poetry in the Bible*   a mass ready to be surveilled, ready to be measured like the sound of water crashing from our eyes   *poetry* limited to islands   *I could not deliver the poem*   instead this threshold of baskets, this wall, door, something to swing open   *I could not deliver* a legacy of outstretched palms   *in the Bible* sound waves measure the ocean floor   in the Navy sound waves measure damage to land&reef systems   in the Pacific   where do you find faith?   the poem pulls you deeper *deliver* a cord hanging deeper *the poem* so deep it is ghost blue&swims to the end of *the poem* a chiefly death rhythms across the room *the Bible* crashing inside *the poem* waters *the poem* deep blue waters I could never find in authorized mor(t)alities *deliver the poem* the brown in our blood the Native in our speech another mat basket *never find* another stranded marine mammal *poetry* might strike *poetry* might kill *the* "no action" *poem* the "no action" poem dies here

after "Sounding" by Kathy Jetñil-Kijiner and Joy Enomoto

SMOKE SCREEN

Noʻu Revilla

Was he a green, long sleeve
jacket & god-fearing man?
On the job, bloodshot.
Marrying metal in his heavy
gloves, bringing justice to his father,
who was also a smoking man.
No bathroom breaks, no helmets, no safe words.
He whistled sugarcane through his neck,
through his unventilated wife,
his chronic black ash daughters.
This is what a burn schedule looks like.
And if believing in god was a respiratory issue,
he was like his father.
Marrying metal to make a family.
At home he smoked before he slept,
in the corner with the door
ajar, cigarette poised like a firstborn:
well-behaved, rehearsed.
Curtains drawn, bedrooms medicated.
He was always burning into something.
Part-dark, part pupils.

For my father, the night was best alone.
When only he could see through
the world and forgive it.

MEMORY AS MISSIONARY POSITION

No'u Revilla

Inside the dress, there is a creature, she
careful

is a cliff in a girl's body.
And the cliff was a lizard once *still*   turned
to rock she gazed too much like she

careful

had a kingdom *inside*.

Inside the dress, holes are cut
    so the cliff can breathe and
        any girl watching
        any girl waiting
        any glint of a girl's

mother's metal scissors can *still* find her –

  careful
there are still pins inside.

To fit a lizard, the jaw of this dress unlocks.
        Fitting sounds like eating and mothers
                tell their daughter to shut their eyes
pins inside the unmarried
pins to decorate
        the insides of a church.
        Girls wear dresses that mothers sew for them.

                        this dress // shroud // napkin // flag

In the 1800s my greatgreatgreatgreatgreat grand
mothers swam to ships
to trade sex for cloth, iron, and mirrors.
        A body for a body.

Did you see yourself in their glass, mother?

Did you cut the shape of your body
        and send it whistling through the ocean?

                        when a cliff becomes altar
and the Pacific
in the name of civilization
is properly dressed

        daughters *inside*
                pine away

the altitude of faith.

INTERGENERATIONAL MEMORY

No'u Revilla

when my feet follow father across the rocks,
    there is always a moment, before sea meets skin
        like a storm, like a house of drums,

when my body is
    ma hope   **ma mua**
    ma mua   **ma hope**

inside me a legacy   'ai pōhaku wāhine   answer

ea, daughters, ea mai loko o ka pō.
    freedom hungry. ua lawa mākou
        i ka pōhaku. we are barefoot and believing
that po'e tell the satisfaction of rocks, tell the satisfaction of gods.

LESSONS IN QUARANTINE

Noʻu Revilla

The second thing I learn is rain.
It falls harder here.
Like the woman at the end
of the road sleeps harder
& locks her doors at night.

Two years ago, with water,
digging stick & a mouthful
of seeds, I walked here.
To the edge of the city.
More mud, bark & branch.
Shades of brown, centuries in the making.
I walked here to live.
The third thing
I learn, this dirt.
This rain sent special for it.
This quelling of madness.
Everything will be green, again.

Yet the first thing,
the very first thing I learn is your hair.
Indomitable, wicked.
The first thing to pry my mouth open
& spit hard for.

CAMILLA AND SERPENTS
Watercolor and Ink
Kanani Miyamoto

This piece was made for a show at Lan Su, the Chinese garden in Portland and was inspired by the change of seasons from winter to spring.

—Kanani Miyamoto

KANANI MIYAMOTO

Kanani Miyamoto (she/her) was born and raised on the island of O`ahu. She is an individual of mixed heritage and identifies most with her Hawaiian and Japanese roots. She currently lives and works in Portland, Oregon.

As an artist, many of Kanani's ideas and themes include, ending the romanticized myths of Pacific Island people. She is focused on ending exotic fantasies built on capitalism and settler colonialism that has damaged the islands and her people. Also important to her work is sharing and celebrating her unique mixed background in our contemporary art world in hopes to represent her community and the beauty of intersectional identities. In her work, many visual elements are pulled from her Buddhist beliefs and Hawaiian heritage. Kanani combines the many philosophies that have formed her identity and the identity of many people from the Hawaiian islands. She wants people to ask more questions and look deeper and harder at visual art. She wants diverse traditional cultural practices embedded into academia. She wants her community represented equally and fairly in the fine art cannon.

Kanani Miyamoto is a practicing artist and curator. She is an instructor at Pacific University, Portland Community College and Pacific Northwest College of Art. She also works with the Right Brain Initiative and Young Audiences as a teaching artist for grades K-12. Kanani organizes and participates in many community arts programs and events.

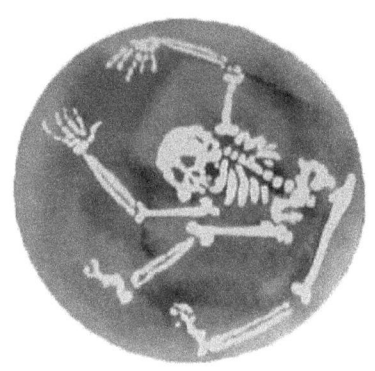

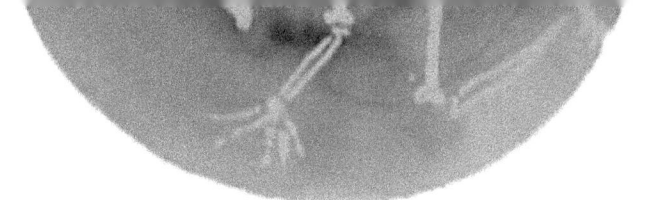
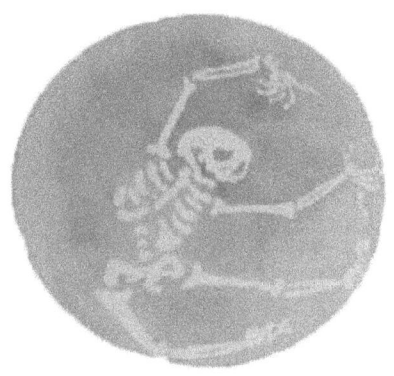

AKAHAI E NĀ HAWAI'I

LŌKAHI A KŪLIKE

'OLU'OLU KA MANA'O

HA'AHA'A KOU KŪLANA

AHONUI A LANAKILA

~~~~

ALOHA MAI E NĀ HAWAI'I

O KE ALOHA NŌ KAU MEA NUI

EŌ MAI E NĀ HAWAI'I

NĀ PUA, NĀ LEI, NĀ MAMO

'ANO'AI NŌ ME KE ALOHA

'ANO'AI NŌ ME KE ALOHA

Make this offering a habit, all persons of Hawai'i:

Obtain oneness, free of duality,

Let thoughts be at ease,

Emptiness is your anchor,

Be with your breath until complete union.

~~~~

Come from ALOHA, all persons of Hawai'i,

If you are fully of ALOHA, you will do great things,

What say you, all people of Hawai'i?

All children, all beloved, all descendants,

Indeed, no one is greater than another, with ALOHA,

Indeed, no one is greater than another, with ALOHA.

ACKNOWLEDGEMENTS

This book was crafted with heart and intention by Malia Guerrero. When a student in my writing and literature classes at Pacific University, Malia spoke and wrote with fierce brilliance about the legends and stories of Hawai'i. A future teacher, she wanted her students to see themselves in the writing they would study with her. In high school Malia did not, as she explains in the opening letter to this book, see herself or her community in the literature she read.

When I asked students, colleagues, and friends about the best way to start the New Ground Book series, the answer came squarely back to Malia and her vision: A book that would be for young people of Hawai'i. It would share the work of poets who would excite and empower them. It would also be a book that modeled how innovative teachers like Malia can create their own materials for their students to read and experience. The outcome is this electric collection.

IMUA, Go Forward is made possible by support from the Stella O. H. Lee Endowment, created by Dr. Timothy Y.C. Choy in honor of his aunt. The endowment promotes access to books through the Pacific University Libraries that focus on the art, history, and culture of Asia and the Pacific. We are also grateful for the support and oversight of Isaac Gilman, Dean of the University Libraries and Editor-in-Chief of Pacific University Press.

The book was designed in many collaborative sessions by Zoe Stanek. Zoe studied Creative Writing and Editing and Publishing with us at Pacific. There were many long nights as Malia, Zoe, and I worked together to honor these writers and this book's mission. As we weighed each word in these poems and studied the artwork you see on these pages, we learned so much.

We offer this first book in the New Ground series to you with awe and respect.

Kathlene Postma
Professor and Series Editor
New Ground Books

The NEW GROUND series publishes books of poetry, short stories, and hybrid forms written by authors of cultures and groups that have been underrepresented in mainstream publishing. We are especially invested in publishing writers who use language to explore their own experiences and cultural traditions in order to strengthen identity and expand understanding.

Pacific University students studying in Editing & Publishing serve in central roles in the editing, designing, promotion, and distribution of books in the series.